AXEL INMAN

Real Life, Real Budget

An Average Person's Guide to Thriving in Expensive Times

Copyright © 2024 by Axel Inman

All rights reserved. No part of this publication may be reproduced, stored or transmitted in any form or by any means, electronic, mechanical, photocopying, recording, scanning, or otherwise without written permission from the publisher. It is illegal to copy this book, post it to a website, or distribute it by any other means without permission.

Axel Inman has no responsibility for the persistence or accuracy of URLs for external or third-party Internet Websites referred to in this publication and does not guarantee that any content on such Websites is, or will remain, accurate or appropriate.

First edition

*This book was professionally typeset on Reedsy.
Find out more at reedsy.com*

Contents

	Introduction	1
1	Assessing Your Financial Situation	2
2	Building a Realistic Budget	7
3	The Psychology of Spending and Saving	13
4	Smart Ways to Cut Everyday Costs	18
5	Debt – How to Manage and Pay It Off	24
6	Building an Emergency Fund – Your Financial Safety Net	30
7	Simple Ways to Reduce Everyday Expenses	36
8	Making the Most of Discounts, Vouchers, and Cashback	42
9	Avoiding Lifestyle Inflation	47
10	Financial Planning for the Future	51
11	Maintaining Your Financial Success	55
12	Conclusion	58
	About the Author	59

Introduction

Why This Book Matters

It's no secret that life's getting more expensive by the day. You've probably noticed it at the supermarket checkout, on your energy bill, and even at the petrol station. From housing to food, everything seems to cost more than it did just a few months ago, and for many of us, that's been a tough pill to swallow.

But here's the thing: while we can't control the cost of living, we can control how we spend and save our hard-earned cash. This book is here to help you do exactly that.

No matter where you're starting from—whether you're struggling to make ends meet or just want to tighten your belt a bit—this book is packed with practical, everyday tips that can make a real difference. And don't worry, I'm not going to tell you to stop buying coffee or give up all the fun things in life. Instead, we'll focus on small, sustainable changes that'll add up to big savings over time.

So, let's dive in. We're going to break things down, step by step, and by the end of this book, you'll be well on your way to saving money like a pro—even in the face of rising costs.

1

Assessing Your Financial Situation

If you're reading this, chances are you're already thinking about how to save money. But before we dive into the juicy tips and tricks, we need to start with the basics: figuring out where your money is going in the first place.

Why You Need to Know Your Numbers

Picture this: you're trying to fill up a leaky bucket. No matter how much water you pour in, it just keeps spilling out. That's exactly what it's like trying to save money without knowing where it's going. You might be earning a decent wage, but if you're spending it faster than it comes in, it'll feel like you're constantly playing catch-up.

The good news? Plugging the leaks in your finances doesn't have to be painful. The first step is simply becoming aware of where your money goes. Once you know that, you can start making smarter choices without feeling like you're missing out.

How to Track Your Spending

Don't worry, I'm not going to suggest anything too complicated. Tracking your spending can be as simple or as detailed as you want it to be. Here are a few options:

- **The Paper Method**: Old-school but effective. Grab a notebook and jot down everything you spend. This works well if you prefer writing things down and keeping it simple.
- **Spreadsheets**: If you like things a bit more organised, you can use a basic spreadsheet to track your income and expenses. List everything you earn in one column and everything you spend in another. It's a simple way to see the bigger picture.
- **Apps**: If you're more tech-savvy, there are plenty of apps out there that do the hard work for you. Apps like Mint, Yolt, or Emma connect to your bank account and automatically categorise your spending, so all you have to do is check in and see where your money is going.

The key here is consistency. You don't need to track every penny forever, but doing it for a month or two will give you a good sense of your habits.

Where Does Your Money Go?

Once you've tracked your spending for a while, you'll start to see some patterns. Chances are, you already know where some of your money goes—rent or mortgage, bills, food. But there might be a few surprises in there too. Maybe it's the daily takeaway coffee that's adding up or that streaming service you forgot you signed up for months ago.

The goal here isn't to make you feel guilty. It's about awareness. Once you know what's happening with your money, you can decide what changes, if any, you want to make.

The First Step to Saving: The 50/30/20 Rule

Now that you've got a clearer picture of your spending, it's time to start thinking about how you'd like to allocate your money. A popular starting point is the **50/30/20 rule**. It's a simple way to break down your spending into three categories:

1. **50% for Needs**: This includes essentials like housing, utilities, groceries, and transport. These are the things you can't do without.
2. **30% for Wants**: These are the fun things—dining out, entertainment, shopping. It's important to leave room for these, so you don't feel like you're depriving yourself.
3. **20% for Savings**: This is the money you'll set aside for the future—whether that's for an emergency fund, paying off debt, or long-term savings.

This rule isn't set in stone, but it gives you a guideline to work from. If your essentials are eating up more than 50%, don't panic—many people are in the same boat, especially with rising costs. The goal is to use this as a framework and adjust where needed.

Quick Win: The Latte Factor

You've probably heard of the "latte factor"—the idea that small, regular purchases, like a daily coffee, add up over time. While I'm not saying you need to give up your coffee, it's worth thinking about those little everyday expenses.

For example, let's say you spend £3 on coffee every day. Over a month, that's £90! If you cut that down to one or two coffees a week, you could save a decent chunk of money without feeling like you're missing out.

Again, the goal isn't to make you feel bad about your spending habits, but to help you find small ways to adjust and save more.

Action Steps

1. **Start Tracking Your Spending**: Whether you choose a notebook, a spreadsheet, or an app, start tracking everything you spend for the next month. The more you know about your habits, the better you'll be able to make changes.
2. **Review Your Subscriptions**: Go through your bank statements and see if there are any services you're paying for but don't use. Cancel anything unnecessary. You'll be surprised how many people forget about those sneaky monthly charges!
3. **Try the 50/30/20 Rule**: If you're ready to start budgeting, try dividing your income according to this rule. Remember, it's flexible—don't stress if your percentages don't line up perfectly.
4. **Find Your Latte Factor**: Look for one small, regular expense that you could cut back on. It might be coffee, takeaway lunches, or even that magazine you never get

around to reading. See if you can trim just a little without feeling like you're sacrificing.

Up Next: Building a Realistic Budget

In the next chapter, we'll take a closer look at budgeting and how to build one that works for your lifestyle. Don't worry—it's easier than you think! Stay tuned for some more practical tips to help you make the most of your money.

2

Building a Realistic Budget

Now that you've started tracking your spending, it's time to take the next step: building a budget. Don't worry, I know the word "budget" can sound a bit boring (or maybe even scary!), but the truth is, budgets don't have to be restrictive. In fact, when done right, they can actually give you more freedom—freedom to spend on the things you enjoy without feeling guilty, and freedom from that nagging feeling of, "Where did all my money go?"

What is a Budget?

At its core, a budget is simply a plan for your money. It helps you decide in advance how you're going to spend, save, and manage what you earn. Think of it like a roadmap—it shows you where your money is going so you can make sure it's heading in the right direction.

The best part? Your budget is totally personal to you. There's no one-size-fits-all approach here, so you can tweak it as much as you need to suit your lifestyle.

The Golden Rule: Spend Less Than You Earn

Let's start with the golden rule of budgeting: **spend less than you earn**. It sounds obvious, but you'd be surprised how easy it is to fall into the trap of spending a little more than you have. With contactless payments, online shopping, and those tempting "buy now, pay later" schemes, it's all too easy to lose track.

A budget helps you make sure that you're living within your means, so you're not relying on credit cards or dipping into your overdraft to get by.

Setting Your Priorities

Before we dive into the numbers, it's important to think about your priorities. What are the things that really matter to you? Maybe it's travelling, saving for a house, or just making sure you have enough money at the end of the month to enjoy a few treats. Whatever it is, your budget should reflect those priorities.

Start by listing your **financial goals**. These might include:

- Paying off debt
- Building an emergency fund
- Saving for a holiday
- Putting money aside for a big purchase (like a new car or house)
- Planning for retirement

Having clear goals will help you stay motivated and give you a reason to stick to your budget. Plus, it'll make it easier to decide where to cut back when necessary.

Breaking Down Your Income and Expenses

Now, let's get into the nitty-gritty of budgeting. There are two main parts to any budget: **income** and **expenses**.

Step 1: Know Your Income

Your income is the money you have coming in each month. For most people, this will be your salary or wages, but it could also include things like:

- Benefits or government support
- Child support
- Income from side gigs or freelance work
- Pensions or other sources of passive income

Make sure you're using your **take-home pay**—that's the amount you get after taxes and any other deductions—because that's what you'll actually have to work with.

Step 2: Know Your Expenses

Now comes the fun part (well, maybe not fun, but definitely important): figuring out your expenses. These are the things you spend money on each month, and they generally fall into two categories:

1. **Fixed Expenses**: These are the costs that stay the same each month, like rent or mortgage payments, utility bills, and insurance premiums.
2. **Variable Expenses**: These can change from month to month, like groceries, transport, and entertainment.

Go back to the tracking you did in Chapter 1 and list out all your expenses. Don't forget the little things—like those cheeky takeaway meals or impulse buys—because they can really add up over time.

Creating Your Budget

Once you've got a clear picture of your income and expenses, it's time to start building your budget. There are lots of different ways to do this, but here's a simple approach that works for most people:

Step 1: Start with Your Essentials

The first thing you need to cover are your **essentials**—these are the things you absolutely can't live without, like housing, utilities, and groceries. Use the **50/30/20 rule** we talked about in Chapter 1 as a guide. Ideally, your essentials should take up no more than 50% of your income, but if they do, don't panic—we'll look at ways to adjust things later on.

Step 2: Allocate for Savings

Next, set aside money for **savings**. Whether it's building up an emergency fund or saving for a specific goal, putting money aside for the future is one of the most important parts of budgeting. Try to aim for at least 20% of your income, but again, if that's not doable right now, that's OK. Start with whatever you can manage and build from there.

Step 3: Give Yourself Some Fun Money

Lastly, we have the fun stuff—your **wants**. This is the 30% of your budget that you can spend on things like dining out, hobbies, and entertainment. It's important to include this in your budget so you don't feel like you're depriving yourself. After all, saving money doesn't mean you have to live like a hermit!

Sticking to Your Budget

Now that you've got a budget, the challenge is sticking to it. Here are a few tips to help you stay on track:

1. **Use Cash or a Debit Card**: If you're tempted to overspend when using a credit card, try sticking to cash or a debit card for everyday purchases. This way, you're only spending money you actually have.
2. **Set Up Direct Debits for Bills and Savings**: Automating your payments can take a lot of the stress out of budgeting. Set up direct debits for your bills and savings, so the money goes out automatically before you have a chance to spend it.
3. **Review Your Budget Regularly**: Life changes, and so should your budget. Review it every few months to make sure it's still working for you, and make adjustments if needed.
4. **Track Your Progress**: Whether you're saving for a holiday or paying off debt, it helps to see how far you've come. Keep track of your progress to stay motivated.

Quick Win: The Envelope System

If you find it hard to stick to a budget, try the **envelope system**. It's an old-school method, but it works! Here's how it goes:

1. Label a few envelopes with categories like "Groceries," "Entertainment," "Dining Out," etc.
2. At the beginning of the month, put the amount of money you've budgeted for each category into the envelope.

3. Once the money's gone, it's gone! You can't dip into other envelopes or spend more than you've allocated.

It's a simple, physical way to keep track of your spending and make sure you're not going over budget.

Action Steps

1. **List Your Income and Expenses**: Use your tracking from Chapter 1 to list out all your income and expenses. Be as detailed as possible.
2. **Create a Budget**: Use the 50/30/20 rule to create a budget that works for you. Don't worry if it's not perfect—budgets are meant to be flexible.
3. **Automate Your Savings**: If possible, set up a direct debit to transfer money into your savings account as soon as you get paid. It's a great way to make sure you're saving consistently.
4. **Try the Envelope System**: If you're struggling to stick to your budget, give the envelope system a go. It's a simple but effective way to manage your spending.

Up Next: The Importance of Financial Habits

In the next chapter, we'll dive into the habits that shape our spending and saving. Understanding why we spend the way we do can be a game-changer when it comes to managing money, so stay tuned!

3

The Psychology of Spending and Saving

Have you ever gone out to buy one thing and ended up with a basket full of extras you didn't really need? Or maybe you've found yourself hitting "Buy Now" on an online order just because it was a good deal? Don't worry, we've all been there! The truth is, a lot of our spending isn't about the stuff we're buying—it's about how we feel when we buy it.

Understanding why we spend the way we do can be a game-changer. It's not just about willpower or self-control; it's about recognising the habits and emotions that drive our choices. Once you know what's going on behind the scenes, you can start making better decisions that align with your financial goals.

Why Do We Overspend?

Overspending is a common problem, and it often has more to do with psychology than with practicality. Here are a few reasons why we tend to spend more than we mean to:

- **Emotional Spending**: Ever heard of "retail therapy"? Some-

times we shop because we're bored, stressed, or even just celebrating. Spending money can give us a temporary mood boost, but it doesn't last. Before we know it, we're feeling guilty and our bank balance is looking a bit worse for wear.
- **The "Deal" Mindset**: Discounts and sales are designed to make us think we're getting a great bargain, even if we're buying things we don't really need. That's why those "Buy One, Get One Half Price" offers are so tempting—they trigger a sense of urgency that can lead to impulsive spending.
- **Lifestyle Creep**: As our income goes up, so do our spending habits. Maybe you got a pay rise and decided to upgrade your car, move to a nicer flat, or start eating out more often. This is called **lifestyle inflation**, and it can sneak up on you, making it harder to save even as your earnings increase.
- **Social Pressures**: Whether it's keeping up with the latest trends or trying to match the spending habits of friends and family, social pressure can push us to buy things we wouldn't otherwise consider.

Building Healthy Money Habits

Now that we know why we overspend, let's talk about how to build habits that work in your favour. The key is to replace unhelpful spending patterns with more intentional behaviours that align with your financial goals.

Tip 1: Wait Before You Buy

One of the simplest tricks to curb impulse spending is to **wait before you buy**. If you see something you really want, give yourself at least 24 hours (or a week, if possible) to think about it. Often, the urge will pass, and you'll realise you don't need it after all. This technique helps separate genuine needs from passing wants.

Tip 2: Use Cash for Discretionary Spending

It's easier to overspend when you're using a card because you don't actually see the money leaving your wallet. Try using cash for things like eating out or buying non-essentials. When the cash is gone, it's gone—there's no tapping a card for just one more thing!

Tip 3: Unsubscribe from Temptation

If your inbox is full of sales alerts and discount codes, it's time to hit the "unsubscribe" button. It's hard to resist buying when you're constantly bombarded with offers. Out of sight, out of mind!

Tip 4: Set Spending Rules

Create a few simple rules to guide your spending. For example, "I'll only buy clothes on sale," or "I won't spend more than £30 on eating out each month." These rules help to cut down on mindless spending and keep you focused on your bigger goals.

Understanding Your Spending Triggers

We all have spending triggers—things that make us want to part with our hard-earned cash. It might be a certain shop, a mood (like feeling bored or stressed), or even a particular person. Take a few minutes to think about your own spending triggers. What situations or emotions tend to lead to unplanned purchases?

Once you've identified your triggers, you can start coming up with strategies to deal with them. For example, if you know you're likely to spend more when you're feeling down, find a healthier way to boost your mood—like going for a walk or calling a friend.

Creating a Money Mindset

A big part of building good money habits is changing the way you think about money. Here are a few mindset shifts that can help:

1. **Think Long-Term**: Instead of focusing on immediate gratification, try to think about the long-term benefits of saving. For example, skipping that daily coffee might not seem like much, but over the course of a year, it could add up to enough for a nice holiday.
2. **Reframe "Cutting Back" as "Choosing Freedom"**: It's easy to feel deprived when you're trying to save money. But instead of thinking about it as cutting back, reframe it as **choosing financial freedom**. Every pound you don't spend now is a pound you're investing in your future.
3. **Celebrate Your Wins**: Saving money isn't always easy, so take time to celebrate your progress! Whether it's paying off a credit card or sticking to your budget for a month, acknowledge your achievements and give yourself credit for the hard work.

Quick Win: Use a "No Spend" Day (or Week)

A great way to reset your spending habits is to have a **No Spend Day**. Pick one day a week where you don't spend any money at all—no takeaway coffees, no snacks, nothing. If you're feeling ambitious, try extending it to a full week. It's a great way to break the habit of mindless spending and to realise just how many things we buy out of habit rather than necessity.

Action Steps

1. **Identify Your Spending Triggers**: Think about the situations or emotions that lead to unplanned spending. Write them down and come up with a strategy to avoid or manage these triggers.
2. **Create a Waiting Period for Big Purchases**: Commit to waiting at least 24 hours before making any non-essential purchases.
3. **Set Up Spending Rules**: Decide on a few simple spending rules to guide your everyday decisions. Stick to these rules to avoid impulse buys.
4. **Try a No Spend Day**: Pick one day this week where you won't spend any money at all. See how it feels and what you learn from the experience.

Up Next: Smart Ways to Cut Everyday Costs

In the next chapter, we'll explore practical ways to cut your everyday expenses without feeling like you're missing out. From energy-saving tips to meal planning hacks, we'll show you how to make your money go further in every area of your life.

4

Smart Ways to Cut Everyday Costs

Cutting back on everyday expenses doesn't have to feel like a chore. In fact, there are plenty of simple, clever ways to save money that you probably won't even notice! From energy bills to groceries, small changes can make a big difference over time, and these savings can go towards more important things—like building an emergency fund, saving for a holiday, or paying off debt.

In this chapter, we'll look at some practical, easy-to-implement strategies to reduce your monthly outgoings without sacrificing your quality of life.

Energy Savings at Home

Energy costs are one of the biggest expenses for most households, especially during the colder months. But with a few adjustments, you can significantly cut your energy usage and lower your bills.

Tip 1: Use a Programmable Thermostat

Heating accounts for a large chunk of your energy bill, so it's worth optimising how and when you use it. A **programmable thermostat** allows you to set your heating to come on only when you're home and to automatically lower the temperature at night or when you're out. You can save a lot of energy (and money) without even thinking about it.

Tip 2: Switch to Energy-Efficient Bulbs

Energy-efficient LED bulbs use up to 90% less energy than traditional incandescent bulbs and last much longer. It's a small upfront cost, but the savings over time are huge. Start by replacing the bulbs in the rooms you use most often—like the kitchen, living room, and bathroom.

Tip 3: Avoid Standby Mode

Leaving your electronics in **standby mode** (like TVs, laptops, and game consoles) still uses energy, even when you're not actively using them. Unplug devices when they're not in use, or invest in smart plugs that automatically cut off power to devices that don't need to be on all the time.

Tip 4: Reduce Your Water Heating Costs

Water heating can also be a big energy drain. Lowering your water heater's temperature by just a few degrees can result in noticeable savings without affecting your comfort. You could also invest in a **low-flow showerhead** to reduce the amount of hot water you use without cutting down your shower time.

Cutting Your Grocery Bill

Food is another major area where costs can add up, especially if you're not keeping a close eye on your spending. But with a bit of planning, you can easily cut your grocery bill without sacrificing quality or flavour.

Tip 1: Plan Your Meals

One of the simplest ways to save money on food is to plan your meals for the week. When you know exactly what you're going to cook, you can create a shopping list that helps you avoid unnecessary impulse buys. Plus, you'll waste less food because you're only buying what you need.

Tip 2: Buy in Bulk (When It Makes Sense)

Buying in bulk can save you a lot of money on items that you use regularly—like pasta, rice, and cleaning supplies. Just make sure that whatever you're buying in bulk is something you'll actually use, and that you have enough storage space.

Tip 3: Cut Back on Convenience Foods

Pre-packaged meals and snacks are convenient, but they come at a premium. You can save a lot by cooking from scratch and preparing your own snacks and lunches. Batch cooking is a great way to save time and money—you can make a big batch of something at the weekend and freeze portions for the rest of the week.

Tip 4: Shop Around for Deals

Don't be loyal to just one supermarket. Prices can vary a lot between different stores, so it's worth shopping around to find the best deals. Many supermarkets now have apps that show their latest offers, so you can plan your shop accordingly.

Transport and Commuting Costs

Transport can be another significant monthly expense, especially if you commute to work. But there are ways to cut these costs without sacrificing convenience.

Tip 1: Use Public Transport or Car Share

If you can, switching to public transport or joining a **car share** scheme can save you money on fuel, parking, and maintenance.

Many cities also have discounts or season passes for public transport, so it's worth checking if this could work for you.

Tip 2: Walk or Cycle When Possible

For shorter journeys, consider walking or cycling instead of driving. Not only is it free, but it's also great for your health. You might be surprised at how many short trips you make by car that could easily be done on foot or by bike.

Tip 3: Keep Your Car in Good Condition

If you do need to drive, make sure your car is running efficiently. Keeping your tyres properly inflated, getting regular services, and driving smoothly (avoiding harsh acceleration and braking) can all help reduce fuel consumption and lower your running costs.

Entertainment on a Budget

Having fun doesn't have to be expensive. There are plenty of ways to enjoy yourself without breaking the bank.

Tip 1: Take Advantage of Free or Low-Cost Activities

Many cities and towns offer free or low-cost events and activities, especially during the summer. From outdoor concerts to museum exhibitions, there's often something going on that doesn't require a big spend. Check your local listings or council website to find out what's on near you.

Tip 2: Use Streaming Services Wisely

If you subscribe to multiple streaming services, you could be paying more than you need to. Try rotating your subscriptions—sign up for one service for a few months, then cancel it and switch to another. This way, you'll always have something new to watch, but you'll only be paying for one service at a time.

Tip 3: Look for Discount Vouchers

Before you go out for a meal, to the cinema, or on a day trip, check if there are any discount vouchers or deals available. Sites like Groupon and VoucherCodes often have great offers that can save you a significant amount.

Reducing Subscription and Membership Costs

It's easy to sign up for subscriptions and memberships without realising how much they're adding to your monthly expenses. Here's how to trim them down.

Tip 1: Review Your Subscriptions Regularly

Take a look at all your subscriptions—streaming services, magazines, apps, gyms, etc.—and ask yourself if you're really getting value from each one. If not, cancel or downgrade them.

Tip 2: Share Subscriptions

Many services offer family or group plans that allow you to share a subscription with friends or family. This can drastically reduce the cost while still giving everyone access.

Tip 3: Pause or Cancel Subscriptions Temporarily

If you're not using a subscription right now, consider pausing or cancelling it. For example, if you're not going to the gym as often, you might be able to freeze your membership for a few months and save some cash.

Quick Win: Embrace the 30-Day Rule

The **30-Day Rule** is a great way to cut down on impulse purchases. If you're thinking about buying something non-essential, wait 30 days before making the decision. If you still want it after that time, go ahead and buy it. But often, you'll find that the urge has passed, and you've saved yourself some money.

Action Steps

1. **Pick One Area to Focus On**: Choose one of the areas above (energy, groceries, transport, entertainment, or subscriptions) and commit to trying out at least one of the tips in that category this week.
2. **Start Meal Planning**: If you're not already doing it, plan your meals for the week and create a shopping list based on that plan. Stick to your list when you go to the supermarket.
3. **Review Your Subscriptions**: Go through your bank statements and make a list of all your subscriptions. Cancel any that you're not using or don't need.
4. **Try a No Spend Challenge**: Challenge yourself to have a **No Spend Day** this week, where you don't spend money on anything non-essential. Use this time to think about where your money usually goes and how you can cut back.

Up Next: Debt – How to Manage and Pay It Off

In the next chapter, we'll dive into strategies for managing and paying off debt. From credit cards to loans, we'll cover practical ways to reduce your debt and start moving towards financial freedom.

5

Debt – How to Manage and Pay It Off

Debt is a reality for many people, and while it can feel overwhelming, it's something you can take control of with the right strategies. Whether it's credit card debt, personal loans, or student loans, getting on top of your repayments and reducing your debt can free up more of your income and reduce financial stress.

In this chapter, we'll explore practical ways to manage and pay off debt, no matter where you're starting from. Remember, the goal is not just to pay off what you owe but also to avoid accumulating more debt in the future.

Understanding Your Debt

Before you can tackle your debt, you need to fully understand what you're dealing with. Gather all your statements and create a list of everything you owe, including:

- **The total amount of each debt** (credit cards, loans, etc.)
- **The interest rates** you're being charged

- **Minimum monthly payments**
- **Payment due dates**

Seeing everything in one place can be a little daunting, but it's important to know where you stand. This list will help you prioritise which debts to tackle first and give you a clearer picture of your financial situation.

Debt Management Strategies

There are several approaches to paying off debt, and the best one for you will depend on your circumstances. Let's explore a few popular methods.

1. The Snowball Method

The **snowball method** involves focusing on paying off your smallest debt first, while making minimum payments on your other debts. Once the smallest debt is cleared, you move on to the next smallest, and so on. The idea is that the psychological boost of paying off debts quickly helps keep you motivated.

How it works:

- List your debts from smallest to largest.
- Pay as much as you can towards the smallest debt while keeping up minimum payments on the others.
- Once the smallest debt is paid off, put that payment amount towards the next smallest debt, and so on.

2. The Avalanche Method

With the **avalanche method**, you focus on paying off the debt with the highest interest rate first. This approach can save you more money in the long run because you'll reduce the amount

of interest you're paying over time.
How it works:

- List your debts from the highest to lowest interest rate.
- Pay as much as possible towards the debt with the highest interest rate, while making minimum payments on the others.
- Once the highest-interest debt is cleared, move on to the next one on the list.

Both the snowball and avalanche methods are effective, so choose the one that feels right for you. If you're motivated by quick wins, the snowball method might suit you best. If you prefer to save the most money on interest, the avalanche method is a better fit.

3. Debt Consolidation

If you're juggling multiple debts, **debt consolidation** could be a good option. This involves taking out a new loan or using a balance transfer credit card to combine all your debts into one. The goal is to secure a lower interest rate, making your monthly payments more manageable.

Be careful, though—debt consolidation doesn't erase your debt. It just simplifies your payments and could reduce your interest charges if you get a good rate. Make sure you do your research and avoid taking on more debt in the process.

4. Negotiate with Your Creditors

If you're struggling to keep up with payments, it's worth contacting your creditors to see if they're willing to negotiate. Many lenders are open to discussing lower interest rates or repayment plans, especially if you explain your financial situation.

You could also explore options like a **balance transfer card** that offers 0% interest for a certain period. This allows you to transfer existing credit card debt to a new card and pay it off interest-free for a limited time—just be sure you can pay it off before the promotional period ends.

Creating a Debt Repayment Plan

Now that you know your options, it's time to create a debt repayment plan that works for you. Here's how to get started:

1. **Set a Clear Goal**: Decide how much you want to pay off each month and when you want to be debt-free. Setting specific, achievable goals will help keep you on track.
2. **Budget for Your Repayments**: Take a look at your budget and identify areas where you can cut back to free up money for debt repayment. This might involve reducing discretionary spending (like eating out or entertainment) or finding ways to lower your bills.
3. **Track Your Progress**: Keep a record of your repayments and celebrate your progress along the way. Every debt you clear is a step towards financial freedom.

Avoiding Debt in the Future

Paying off debt is only half the battle—staying out of debt is just as important. Here are some tips to avoid falling back into old habits:

- **Build an Emergency Fund**: One of the most effective ways to avoid future debt is to have an emergency fund in place. Aim to save at least three to six months' worth of living

expenses. This will give you a buffer for unexpected costs (like car repairs or medical bills) without relying on credit.
- **Use Credit Wisely**: Credit cards can be useful tools if used responsibly. If you do use credit, try to pay off the balance in full each month to avoid interest charges. Only use credit for things you can afford to pay off right away.
- **Stick to a Budget**: Having a budget in place will help you manage your money and avoid overspending. Make sure to include a category for savings, even if it's a small amount each month.

Dealing with High-Interest Debt

If you're struggling with high-interest debt (like payday loans or credit card balances), it's important to prioritise paying these off as quickly as possible. The longer you carry a balance on high-interest debt, the more you'll end up paying in interest.

One option is to use a **debt management plan** through a non-profit organisation, which can help you negotiate lower interest rates or extended repayment terms. This can make your monthly payments more affordable while helping you get out of debt faster.

Quick Win: Automate Your Debt Payments

One of the easiest ways to stay on top of your debt repayments is to set up automatic payments. This ensures you never miss a payment and helps you avoid late fees. You can automate the minimum payments on all your debts and then make extra payments manually when you can.

Action Steps

1. **Choose Your Debt Repayment Method**: Decide whether the snowball or avalanche method is best for you and start making extra payments towards your priority debt.
2. **Set Up Automatic Payments**: Automate your debt repayments to ensure you're never late and avoid interest charges or fees.
3. **Create a Debt-Free Goal**: Write down your goal for becoming debt-free, including a target date and the monthly amount you need to pay to reach it.
4. **Review Your Budget**: Find areas where you can cut back to free up money for debt repayment. Even small adjustments can make a big difference over time.

Up Next: Building an Emergency Fund

In the next chapter, we'll focus on one of the most important steps in achieving financial stability—building an emergency fund. We'll look at how much you should save, where to keep your emergency fund, and how to build it up even if you're starting with a tight budget.

6

Building an Emergency Fund – Your Financial Safety Net

An emergency fund is one of the most important financial tools you can have. It acts as a buffer between you and unexpected expenses, allowing you to avoid taking on debt when life throws you a curveball. Whether it's a surprise car repair, medical expense, or sudden job loss, having an emergency fund ensures that you're prepared.

In this chapter, we'll explore why having an emergency fund is crucial, how much you should aim to save, and practical steps to get started, even if money is tight.

Why You Need an Emergency Fund

Life is unpredictable, and it's impossible to know when an unexpected expense might arise. An emergency fund gives you the peace of mind that you'll be able to handle whatever comes your way without derailing your finances.

Here's why it's important:

- **Avoid Debt**: Without an emergency fund, unexpected expenses often lead to credit card debt or loans, which can take a long time to pay off and come with high-interest rates.
- **Financial Security**: Knowing you have a cushion to fall back on reduces financial anxiety and allows you to handle emergencies calmly.
- **Control Over Your Finances**: Instead of scrambling to find money or relying on credit, you'll have the funds available to cover emergencies and continue focusing on your financial goals.

How Much Should You Save?

The amount you should save in your emergency fund depends on your personal circumstances. A general rule of thumb is to aim for **three to six months' worth of living expenses**. This gives you enough to cover your essentials (like rent, bills, and groceries) if you lose your income or face a large unexpected cost.

Three Months' Expenses: A good starting point for most people, especially if you have a stable job and minimal debt.

Six Months' Expenses: Ideal for those with less predictable income (such as freelancers), those in industries prone to job loss, or those who prefer extra security.

If saving three to six months' expenses feels daunting, don't worry—start small and build up gradually. Even having £500 to £1,000 saved can make a huge difference in an emergency.

Where to Keep Your Emergency Fund

The key to an effective emergency fund is that it needs to be **accessible** but not so easy to access that you're tempted to dip into it for non-emergencies. Here are some options for where to keep your fund:

1. High-Interest Savings Account

A **high-interest savings account** is a great option for your emergency fund. It allows your money to grow a little while still being easy to access. Look for an account with no fees and easy withdrawal options.

2. Easy Access Savings Account

If you prefer to prioritise accessibility over interest rates, an **easy access savings account** could be a better fit. While the interest rates might be lower, you'll have immediate access to your funds if an emergency arises.

3. Cash ISA (Individual Savings Account)

A **Cash ISA** allows you to save up to a certain amount each year tax-free. While ISAs can be a bit more difficult to access than a regular savings account, they offer tax benefits and can be a useful place to store your emergency fund.

How to Build Your Emergency Fund

Building an emergency fund can feel like a big task, especially if your budget is tight. But remember, every little bit helps! Here are some practical steps to get you started:

1. Set a Realistic Savings Goal

Start by setting a small, achievable goal, like saving £500. Once you hit that, aim for £1,000. Breaking it down into smaller milestones makes the process feel more manageable.

2. Automate Your Savings

Set up an automatic transfer from your current account to your savings account each payday. Even if it's just £10 or £20 a month, automating the process ensures you're consistently building your emergency fund without having to think about it.

3. Cut Back on Discretionary Spending

Look for areas in your budget where you can cut back, even temporarily, to free up money for your emergency fund. Consider reducing expenses like takeaways, subscriptions, or clothing purchases for a few months.

4. Use Windfalls Wisely

Whenever you receive extra money—whether it's a tax refund, birthday money, or a bonus from work—consider putting some or all of it into your emergency fund. Windfalls are a great way to make significant progress without affecting your regular budget.

5. Sell Unwanted Items

Consider decluttering your home and selling unwanted items online or at a car boot sale. Not only will you clear out space, but you'll also make some extra cash to put towards your emergency fund.

When to Use Your Emergency Fund

It's important to use your emergency fund **only for true emergencies**. Here's a simple rule to follow: if it's something that needs to be dealt with immediately and affects your essential needs (like housing, food, or health), it's an emergency.

Examples of emergencies include:

- **Medical bills**
- **Car repairs**

- **Unexpected home repairs**
- **Job loss or reduced income**

Non-emergencies (like holidays, gadgets, or new furniture) should be saved for separately or included in your regular budget.

Rebuilding Your Emergency Fund

Once you've used your emergency fund, it's important to rebuild it as soon as possible. Follow the same steps as before—set a goal, automate your savings, and look for extra ways to add to your fund. Remember, having a fully funded emergency account gives you financial peace of mind.

Quick Win: Open a High-Interest Savings Account

One quick action you can take today is to open a high-interest savings account for your emergency fund. Compare different options online and choose one that offers both accessibility and a competitive interest rate. Once your account is set up, start transferring any extra money into it.

Action Steps

1. **Set a Savings Goal**: Decide how much you want to save in your emergency fund and set an initial goal (e.g., £500).
2. **Open a Savings Account**: If you don't already have one, open a high-interest or easy-access savings account to hold your emergency fund.
3. **Automate Your Savings**: Set up an automatic transfer to

your emergency fund each payday, even if it's just a small amount.
4. **Find Ways to Cut Back**: Review your budget and look for areas where you can temporarily cut back to boost your savings.

Up Next: Simple Ways to Reduce Everyday Expenses

In the next chapter, we'll dive into specific ways you can reduce your day-to-day expenses. From groceries to utilities, we'll explore practical strategies for cutting back and saving more money without sacrificing your quality of life.

7

Simple Ways to Reduce Everyday Expenses

Everyday expenses can add up quickly, often without us even realising it. However, with some simple strategies and a little effort, you can significantly reduce your monthly spending without feeling deprived. Whether it's on groceries, utilities, or transportation, cutting back on day-to-day costs can free up more of your income for savings or other financial goals.

In this chapter, we'll cover practical tips to help you reduce your everyday expenses. The great thing is that many of these changes are small but have a big impact over time.

Groceries – Saving at the Supermarket

One of the largest regular expenses for most households is groceries. With food prices on the rise, being smart about how and where you shop can save you a lot of money.

1. Plan Your Meals

Meal planning is one of the most effective ways to save on groceries. By planning your meals for the week ahead, you can create a shopping list of exactly what you need, helping you avoid impulse buys or unnecessary items.

How to get started:

- Plan meals around items on sale or things you already have in your pantry.
- Choose recipes that use similar ingredients to reduce waste.
- Cook in batches and freeze meals to save time and money throughout the week.

2. Buy in Bulk

For non-perishable items like pasta, rice, and tinned goods, buying in bulk can save you money in the long run. Just be sure you have enough storage space and that you're buying items you'll use before they expire.

3. Shop Around

Different supermarkets often have different prices for the same products. If you have the time, shopping at multiple stores or checking prices online before you go can help you find the best deals.

Many people also find savings by shopping at discount stores like Aldi or Lidl, which often carry the same products at lower prices compared to the big-name supermarkets.

4. Use Own-Brand Products

Supermarket own-brand products are usually just as good as name-brand ones but cost significantly less. Try swapping out a few branded items in your shopping trolley for the store's own version—you may not even notice the difference in quality, but you will in the price.

5. Don't Shop When You're Hungry

It sounds simple, but shopping when you're hungry can lead

to impulse buys and overspending on snacks and treats. Have a snack before heading to the supermarket, and stick to your list.

Utilities – Cutting Down on Bills

Utilities are another major monthly expense, but there are ways to reduce your bills without making drastic changes to your lifestyle.

1. Switch Providers

One of the easiest ways to save money on utilities like gas, electricity, and broadband is to compare providers regularly. Many people stay on the same tariff for years, but switching can lead to substantial savings.

Use comparison websites to find the best deals and switch to a cheaper tariff if possible. Some energy companies also offer incentives or discounts for switching.

2. Use Energy Efficiently

Reducing your energy consumption is another way to cut down on bills. Here are some simple ways to use less energy at home:

- **Turn off appliances** when not in use, including electronics and lights.
- **Wash clothes at lower temperatures**—30°C is often enough to clean clothes well.
- **Install energy-efficient light bulbs**, which last longer and use less electricity.
- **Reduce heating costs** by using draft excluders, closing curtains at night, and lowering your thermostat by a degree or two.

3. Take Advantage of Off-Peak Hours

If your energy provider offers different rates for peak and off-peak hours, try to use energy-intensive appliances (like washing machines and dishwashers) during off-peak times to save money.

Transportation – Cutting Costs on Commuting

Transportation costs, whether it's fuel, public transport, or car maintenance, can take a big bite out of your budget. Here are a few ways to reduce your transportation expenses.

1. Car Share or Use Public Transport

If you commute to work or drive regularly, consider car sharing with colleagues or friends. Splitting the cost of fuel and parking can lead to significant savings over time. Alternatively, using public transport can often be cheaper than driving, especially when factoring in parking fees and fuel.

2. Maintain Your Car

Regular maintenance can help your car run more efficiently and prevent costly repairs. Simple things like keeping your tyres properly inflated, getting regular oil changes, and addressing minor issues before they become bigger problems can save you money in the long term.

3. Walk or Cycle for Short Journeys

For shorter trips, consider walking or cycling instead of driving. Not only will you save on fuel, but you'll also get some exercise in the process. If cycling to work is an option, many employers offer the **Cycle to Work scheme**, which provides a tax-efficient way to buy a bike.

Entertainment – Have Fun Without Overspending

We all need to relax and have fun, but entertainment costs can easily add up. Whether it's going out for dinner, taking the family to the cinema, or subscribing to multiple streaming services, entertainment is an area where small changes can make a big difference.

1. Cut Back on Subscriptions

Take a look at any subscriptions you have, whether it's streaming services, magazines, or apps. Are you really using them all? Consider cancelling any subscriptions you don't use regularly, or rotating services—subscribe to one at a time and switch every few months to keep things fresh without paying for multiple services at once.

2. Look for Free or Low-Cost Activities

There are plenty of free or low-cost ways to enjoy yourself, whether it's a day out at a local park, attending a free event, or visiting a museum with no admission fee. Many towns and cities have plenty of budget-friendly options if you take the time to look.

3. Limit Eating Out

Eating out can be a treat, but it can also be expensive. Consider cutting back on how often you eat out and cooking more at home instead. When you do go out, look for deals or special offers, such as early bird menus or using apps that offer discounts.

Quick Win: Review Your Subscriptions

Take five minutes to review your monthly subscriptions. Cancel anything you're not using regularly, and consider downgrading to a cheaper plan or sharing accounts with friends or family where possible.

Action Steps

1. **Plan Your Meals**: Start meal planning for the week ahead and create a shopping list based on your plan.
2. **Switch Energy Providers**: Use a comparison website to check if you can get a better deal on your utilities.
3. **Review Transportation Costs**: Consider car sharing, using public transport, or walking for short journeys to save on fuel.
4. **Cut Unnecessary Subscriptions**: Review your entertainment subscriptions and cancel any you're not using regularly.

Up Next: Making the Most of Discounts, Vouchers, and Cashback

In the next chapter, we'll explore how to take full advantage of discounts, vouchers, and cashback offers to save even more on your purchases. With a bit of effort, you can make these savings strategies part of your everyday routine and watch the benefits add up.

8

Making the Most of Discounts, Vouchers, and Cashback

Who doesn't love a bargain? Discounts, vouchers, and cashback schemes can be powerful tools for saving money on everyday purchases, provided you use them wisely. From loyalty cards to online cashback offers, learning how to navigate these systems can help you keep more money in your pocket.

In this chapter, we'll explore the different types of discounts available, where to find vouchers, and how to maximise cashback schemes without falling into the trap of buying things you don't need.

Finding Discounts – Savvy Shopping

It's no secret that discounts are everywhere, but knowing how to find and use them effectively is key to getting the best deals. Whether you're shopping online or in-store, here are some ways to spot savings opportunities.

1. Shop the Sales

Major sales events like **Black Friday**, **Boxing Day**, or **end-**

of-season sales are great opportunities to pick up items at a discounted price. However, it's important not to get swept up in the hype. Make a list of what you need and stick to it—sales are only a saving if you were going to buy the item anyway.

2. Use Price Comparison Sites

Before buying anything online, use a **price comparison website** to check if you can get it cheaper elsewhere. These sites compare prices across multiple retailers and can highlight special deals or offers. A few popular ones include **PriceRunner** and **Google Shopping**.

3. Sign Up for Store Newsletters

Many retailers offer a discount for signing up to their newsletters—usually 10% to 20% off your first purchase. While it's not wise to clutter your inbox with dozens of emails, signing up for your favourite stores' newsletters can give you early access to sales and special offers.

4. Look for Student, NHS, or Military Discounts

If you're a student, NHS worker, or in the military, you may be eligible for exclusive discounts. Websites like **UNiDAYS** and **Blue Light Card** provide discounts for these groups at a variety of retailers, from clothing to tech.

Using Vouchers – Extra Savings at Your Fingertips

Vouchers (or coupons) can offer significant savings, but it's important to use them strategically. Here's how to make the most of vouchers without falling into the trap of buying things just because they're on offer.

1. Search for Online Vouchers

Before making any purchase online, do a quick search for a voucher code. Websites like **VoucherCodes** and **Honey** provide codes for discounts, free delivery, or money off your first order. If you're a regular shopper at certain stores, installing a browser extension like **Honey** can automatically find and apply codes at checkout.

2. Collect Paper Vouchers

Supermarkets often provide paper vouchers with your receipt or through loyalty schemes. Don't throw them away—take a moment to check if they're for products you actually buy. Many supermarkets also offer personalised vouchers based on your previous shopping habits, which can be particularly useful.

3. Use Multi-Buy Offers Wisely

Multi-buy offers, such as "buy one, get one free" (BOGOF), can seem like great deals, but only if you need the items. Before grabbing a multi-buy offer, ask yourself if you'll actually use both items or if it'll just sit in a cupboard. Multi-buys are great for essentials like toilet paper or cleaning products, but be cautious with perishable goods.

Cashback – Earn Money as You Spend

Cashback schemes allow you to earn back a percentage of your purchase, either as cash or store credit. While it might only seem like a small amount, cashback can add up significantly over time, especially if you use it regularly.

1. Join Cashback Websites

Websites like **TopCashback** and **Quidco** partner with retailers to offer cashback on purchases. By clicking through to the retailer's website via these platforms, you can earn a percentage back on what you spend. It's simple to use, and over time, you can accumulate a fair bit of money.

2. Cashback Credit Cards

Some credit cards offer cashback on every purchase. While these can be a good way to earn a little extra, it's important to pay off your balance in full every month. The interest on credit card debt will quickly wipe out any cashback you earn if you don't pay it off.

3. Cashback on Bills

Certain utility providers, broadband companies, and even insurance companies offer cashback when you switch to their service. When comparing prices for utilities or insurance, check if cashback is available—it can make switching providers even more worthwhile.

Avoiding the Pitfalls of Discounts and Cashback

While discounts, vouchers, and cashback are great tools for saving, they can also encourage unnecessary spending. Here are some common pitfalls to watch out for:

1. Don't Buy Just for the Discount

It's easy to get excited about a discount and buy something you don't really need. Before making a purchase, ask yourself if you would still buy the item if it wasn't on sale. If the answer is no, put it back.

2. Watch Out for Expiring Cashback

Cashback often has an expiration date, meaning you'll need to claim it within a certain period or risk losing it. Set a reminder to ensure you don't miss out on claiming your cashback.

3. Check the Fine Print

Make sure you understand the terms and conditions of any discount or cashback offer. Some discounts may only apply to certain products, or there may be a minimum spend required to claim the cashback.

Quick Win: Install a Cashback Browser Extension

A simple way to start saving immediately is by installing a cashback browser extension like **Honey** or **TopCashback**. These extensions automatically find discounts and cashback opportunities when you shop online, saving you both time and money.

Action Steps

1. **Sign Up for a Cashback Website**: Join a cashback platform like **TopCashback** or **Quidco** and start earning cashback on your everyday purchases.
2. **Check for Vouchers Before Shopping**: Before making any purchase online or in-store, check if there's a voucher code or paper voucher you can use for extra savings.
3. **Review Your Discount Options**: Sign up for newsletters from your favourite stores to stay informed of upcoming sales and discounts.

Up Next: Avoiding Lifestyle Inflation

In the next chapter, we'll explore the concept of lifestyle inflation—how as your income increases, so do your expenses—and how to resist the urge to spend more just because you can. Learn how to stay financially grounded as your income grows.

9

Avoiding Lifestyle Inflation

Lifestyle inflation refers to the tendency to increase spending as your income grows. While it's natural to want to enjoy the benefits of a pay rise or financial windfall, lifestyle inflation can prevent you from saving or investing in your future. In this chapter, we'll explore ways to avoid the trap of spending more just because you're earning more.

What is Lifestyle Inflation?

Lifestyle inflation happens when you start to spend more money as soon as you have more of it. This often means upgrading your car, moving to a more expensive home, or spending more on clothes, entertainment, and dining out. The issue with lifestyle inflation is that it can leave you with little to no extra savings, even if you're earning significantly more than before.

Signs You're Experiencing Lifestyle Inflation

- You upgrade your lifestyle (home, car, gadgets) whenever you get a raise.
- Your expenses increase in line with your income.
- You don't see a significant change in your savings despite higher earnings.
- You feel like you're living paycheck to paycheck, even with a larger income.

How to Combat Lifestyle Inflation

1. Set Savings Goals First

Before you start increasing your spending, set financial goals that prioritise saving. This could be building an emergency fund, increasing your retirement savings, or putting money towards a big goal like buying a house. By setting these goals first, you'll ensure that extra income goes towards securing your future, not just funding short-term wants.

2. Increase Your Savings Rate

As your income increases, consider raising your savings rate rather than your spending. For example, if you're currently saving 10% of your income, increase this to 15% or 20% when you receive a pay rise. This will help you accumulate wealth over time while still allowing you to enjoy some of the benefits of your higher earnings.

3. Delay Major Purchases

When you get a raise, it can be tempting to celebrate by making a big purchase. Instead of rushing into it, wait for a few months. This gives you time to assess whether the purchase is really necessary or if it's just a fleeting desire. Delaying purchases can also give you time to save for them, reducing the need for credit or loans.

4. Maintain Your Current Lifestyle

One of the simplest ways to avoid lifestyle inflation is to keep your spending at the same level, even as your income rises. This doesn't mean you have to deprive yourself, but it encourages thoughtful spending. By keeping your lifestyle in check, you can divert more of your income into savings, investments, or paying down debt.

5. Automate Your Savings

Set up automatic transfers to your savings account or investment fund whenever you get paid. By automating your savings, you remove the temptation to spend the money, making it easier to stick to your financial goals.

6. Focus on Value, Not Price

Instead of focusing on buying the most expensive items, look for things that offer the best value for your money. This mindset can help you avoid unnecessary spending and encourage you to make thoughtful purchases that provide long-term satisfaction.

Quick Win: Automate a Savings Increase

The next time you get a raise, set up an automatic transfer to your savings or investment account that reflects a percentage of the raise. This ensures that you save more without even having to think about it.

Action Steps

1. **Set a New Savings Goal**: Whether it's for an emergency fund or retirement, make a plan for how you'll allocate extra income towards your savings.
2. **Delay a Major Purchase**: If you're considering a big purchase, wait a few months and assess if it's still necessary.
3. **Increase Your Savings Rate**: With your next raise, aim to save at least 50% of the increase to avoid lifestyle inflation.

Up Next: Financial Planning for the Future

In the next chapter, we'll dive into how to set financial goals and plan ahead for big expenses like retirement, property ownership, and education costs. As you manage your day-to-day spending, it's equally important to plan for the future.

10

Financial Planning for the Future

Saving money isn't just about cutting back on everyday expenses—it's also about planning for the future. Whether it's for retirement, your children's education, or a home, setting long-term financial goals is crucial for building wealth and financial security.

In this chapter, we'll discuss key aspects of financial planning, including retirement savings, investments, and preparing for life's big expenses.

Planning for Retirement

One of the biggest financial goals for most people is saving for retirement. The earlier you start, the easier it will be to reach your target.

1. Start a Pension Fund Early

If your employer offers a pension scheme, make sure you're contributing enough to take full advantage of any employer match. If you're self-employed, consider setting up a personal pension and making regular contributions. The power of compound interest means that the earlier you start, the more your money will grow over time.

2. Increase Contributions Over Time

As your income grows, increase your pension contributions to ensure you're building a healthy retirement fund. Even small increases over time can make a big difference when compounded over decades.

3. Consider ISAs

For tax-efficient savings, consider investing in an **Individual Savings Account (ISA)**. ISAs allow you to save or invest money without paying tax on the interest, dividends, or capital gains. You can choose between a cash ISA for low-risk savings or a stocks and shares ISA for long-term growth.

Investing for the Future

Investing can be an excellent way to grow your wealth, but it's important to understand the risks involved. If you're new to investing, here are some key principles to keep in mind.

1. Start Small

If you're new to investing, it's wise to start small. You don't need to invest large sums of money straight away. Begin with an amount you're comfortable with and gradually increase it as you learn more.

2. Diversify Your Investments

Diversification is key to managing risk in your investment portfolio. Spread your investments across different asset classes (such as stocks, bonds, and property) and sectors to minimise the impact of any single investment underperforming.

3. Invest for the Long Term

Investing is a long-term game. Avoid the temptation to chase quick returns, and instead, focus on building a diversified portfolio that will grow steadily over time. Stay patient, even during market downturns, and avoid making impulsive decisions based on short-term fluctuations.

Preparing for Major Life Expenses

Throughout your life, you'll encounter several major expenses—buying a home, paying for education, or starting a family. Planning ahead for these expenses can reduce financial stress and help you achieve your goals without taking on unnecessary debt.

1. Save for a House Deposit

If you're planning to buy a house, start saving for a deposit as early as possible. Aim for at least 10% of the property's value, but more is even better. Consider opening a **Lifetime ISA**, which allows you to save for a house deposit with the added benefit of government bonuses.

2. Plan for Children's Education

If you have children or plan to have them in the future, consider saving for their education early. University fees and living costs can be significant, and having a savings fund in place can make a big difference when the time comes.

3. Build an Emergency Fund

Having an emergency fund is crucial for financial security. Aim to save three to six months' worth of living expenses to cover unexpected events like job loss, medical bills, or urgent home repairs.

Quick Win: Open an ISA

If you don't already have one, consider opening an ISA. It's a tax-efficient way to save or invest money, and over time, it can help you build wealth without losing money to taxes.

Action Steps

1. **Review Your Pension Contributions**: Make sure you're contributing enough to your pension fund to take full advantage of employer matches or build a solid retirement fund.
2. **Start an Investment Plan**: If you haven't already, consider starting an investment plan. Even a small monthly contribution can grow significantly over time.
3. **Set Up an Emergency Fund**: If you don't already have one, start building an emergency fund to cover unexpected expenses.

Up Next: Maintaining Your Financial Success

Now that you've planned for the long term, let's talk about how to stay on top of your finances as life changes. The final chapter will explore how to maintain your financial success and ensure you don't fall back into old habits.

11

Maintaining Your Financial Success

Once you've developed smart saving habits and improved your financial situation, the challenge is maintaining that success over time. Financial discipline requires ongoing attention and effort, but with the right mindset, you can continue to build on the progress you've made.

In this final chapter, we'll cover strategies to help you stay on track, avoid setbacks, and continue making smart financial decisions well into the future.

1. Review Your Finances Regularly

It's important to check in on your finances regularly. Set aside time each month to review your spending, savings, and financial goals. This will help you stay on top of your budget and make adjustments as needed.

2. Adjust Your Budget as Life Changes

Your financial situation is likely to change over time. Whether it's a new job, a growing family, or an unexpected expense, it's important to adjust your budget accordingly. Be flexible, and remember that your financial goals may evolve as your circumstances change.

3. Keep Learning

Financial literacy is an ongoing process. Continue to educate yourself about saving, investing, and managing money. Read books, listen to podcasts, or attend workshops to stay informed about personal finance topics.

4. Celebrate Milestones

Achieving financial goals takes time and effort, so don't forget to celebrate your progress. Whether it's paying off debt, reaching a savings target, or sticking to your budget for a full year, take the time to acknowledge your accomplishments.

5. Avoid Financial Complacency

It can be easy to become complacent once you've reached a certain level of financial success, but it's important to remain disciplined. Continue saving, investing, and making smart financial decisions, even when things are going well.

Quick Win: Schedule a Financial Review

Take a few minutes to schedule a regular financial review—whether it's monthly, quarterly, or annually. This simple step can help you stay on track and avoid financial surprises.

Action Steps

1. **Set a Review Schedule**: Commit to reviewing your finances regularly, whether it's monthly or quarterly.
2. **Continue Your Financial Education**: Keep learning about personal finance through books, podcasts, and courses.
3. **Celebrate Your Progress**: Take a moment to celebrate the financial milestones you've achieved, and use them as motivation to continue your financial journey.

12

Conclusion

A New Financial Beginning

Congratulations on reaching the end of this journey! By now, you've learned practical strategies for saving money, cutting costs, and building a more secure financial future. Whether it's finding small savings in everyday expenses or planning for major life events, the steps you take today will help you achieve your long-term goals.

Remember, financial success is not about being perfect—it's about making progress. With the tools and knowledge you've gained from this book, you're well on your way to creating a brighter financial future for yourself and your family.

Keep going, stay disciplined, and most importantly, enjoy the rewards of your hard work!

About the Author

Axel Inman is a passionate advocate for helping everyday people take control of their finances, especially during tough economic times. With a deep understanding of the challenges faced by ordinary households, Axel has made it his mission to simplify personal finance for those who don't have time to decode complex jargon or wade through financial theories. His writing is practical, accessible, and focused on real-life solutions for normal people who just want to stretch their money further without sacrificing their lifestyle.

Axel draws on years of personal experience navigating financial struggles in a time of rising costs, offering readers not only his insights but also encouragement to succeed. He knows that managing money can feel overwhelming, but his down-to-earth advice and easy-to-apply strategies make financial freedom feel achievable for anyone, no matter their starting point. His approach to frugal living and smart budgeting has resonated with readers looking for straightforward, no-nonsense guidance.

You can connect with me on:

◼ https://www.facebook.com/AxelInmanAuthor

www.ingramcontent.com/pod-product-compliance
Lightning Source LLC
Chambersburg PA
CBHW030048230526
45471CB00003B/997